William Roscoe Thayer

Poems, New And Old

William Roscoe Thayer

Poems, New And Old

ISBN/EAN: 9783744651769

Printed in Europe, USA, Canada, Australia, Japan

Cover: Foto ©Thomas Meinert / pixelio.de

More available books at **www.hansebooks.com**

POEMS, NEW AND OLD

BY

WILLIAM ROSCOE THAYER

BOSTON AND NEW YORK
HOUGHTON, MIFFLIN AND COMPANY
The Riverside Press, Cambridge
1894

The Riverside Press, Cambridge, Mass., U. S. A.
Electrotyped and Printed by H. O. Houghton and Company.

TO ELIZABETH.

Set her among the angels! let her shine a star!
   Nay, call her woman, never more divine
Than when she walks the levels where our human long-
      ings are,
   And lightens up the prison where we pine.

Be angel to my worship! be star my steps to lead
   From Earth's deep gloom to thy radiance above!
The daily inspiration of thine influence I need,
   But oh! be simply woman to my love.

CONTENTS.

POEMS.

HALÎD.

A TALE TOLD BY A STRANGE MAN AT THE TOMBS OF
THE KHALÎFS, NEAR CAIRO, JANUARY 23, 1887.

" I am Halîd of Mosûl, the man unpermitted
    to die.
Do you start? would you laugh? do you peer for
    the madman's flash in my eye?
Nay — that is pity, not fear nor contempt that
    has soften'd your cheek ;
I am dumb to the heartless who mock, to the ears
    of compassion I speak.
I was born in the valley the Tigris loves, in the
    reign of Harûn,
When the land was fragrant with poets' breath,
    and the crescent moon
Rose out of Indus and sank in the waves of the
    Western Sea,
And never a man that it blanch'd but bow'd unto
    Allah the knee.
In the smile of the gracious Khalîf we throve ;
    our zenith was then

When the brave with the scimitar wrought for
    fame, and the wise with the pen!
I was young, I was proud, and I lov'd — ah,
    better for me had I died!
Have you felt the first soft dovelike kiss from
    the lips of a bride?
Have you seen the roses of Shiraz ablush at the
    wooing of spring?
In the almond-groves of Bushire have you heard
    the bulbul sing?
Have you tasted the honey of Ramleh's bees? —
    But you never can know
The beauty of Leila, my bride who vanish'd
    long ages ago!
Lilies are fair and white, and fragrant is spike-
    nard prest,
But oh! the lilies, and oh! the spice in that gar-
    den, her breast!

"One morn I arose and went to the mosque
    my devotions to pay —
Had not Allah been kind beyond thanking, to
    me? — I met on the way
Hassan, the friend of my youth, my brother, my
    comrade in joy,
With the strength of a man, and a seraph's face,
    and the mirth of a boy;
He, too, newly-wedded, still glow'd at the thought
    of his Fatima's kiss,
And we talk'd as we went, as lovers will talk, of
    our brides and our bliss.

But just at the door of the mosque, the words on
    his lips half-said,
Without warning or sigh on the cruel step my
    Hassan fell dead.
' A sudden snap of the chords of a heart unus'd
    to the strain
' Of the music of Love,' quoth a leech ; ' joy kill-
    eth as surely as pain.'
My Paradise pass'd like a mist, I was scorch'd
    by the fires of Hell,
And they dried the torrent of grief that had
    gush'd from my lids when he fell.

"I had come to the mosque to give thanks,
    from its threshold I turn'd me in wrath
And wander'd, it reck'd me not whither, for
    demons beleaguer'd my path.
First, Love bewilder'd would cry for his friend,
    then Anger would smite,
And I long'd to avenge on the Angel of Death
    his coward despite ;
Then I mus'd, ' What a pitiful world is this !
    what profits our life,
' When neither our Joy nor our Love is shielded
    from Azrael's knife ?
' To Allah we pray as our God, almighty we call
    Him, and just, —
' Was it righteous to stifle the lips of my friend
    with a handful of dust ?
' If Joy be the heavenly guerdon that God on the
    faithful bestows

'Why smites He the happy on earth? If His
    power no obstacle knows
'Why leaves He the youthful and good to be
    slain, and the wicked to flee?
'Why spares He the old over-ripe? Is Death
    more mighty than He?
'Then Death will I worship, not impotent Allah,
    and him will implore
'To forget for awhile that I live, and to pass un-
    enter'd my door.'

"Thus darkling I sought my abode, and Leila
    I drew to my breast;
My fingers tenderly stray'd in her hair, and her
    cheeks I caress'd,
But joy did not wake at the touch, there was gall
    in her kisses sweet,
For I heard a voice in my heart, 'Her bosom
    may cease to beat —
'The bride you enfold in your arms, at a twink-
    ling may turn to clay —
'Ere you smooth her tresses again, yourself may
    be summon'd away!
'Fool! life and delight are not yours, but the
    plaything of whimsical Death;
'The Palace of Love where you dwell is a bubble
    to burst at a breath!'
So I liv'd as a stranger to joy, tho' the trappings
    of joy were mine:
When wormwood embitters the tongue, what
    savor hath honey, or wine?

And over the world there lower'd a pall, as at an
    eclipse,
And I heard only dirges in song, and wails upon
    laughing lips.
Wherever I walk'd there lengthen'd before me
    the shadow black
Of the wings of the Angel of Death, and I
    fear'd to turn and look back,
Out of dread for his terrible face, and his arm
    uplifted to slay :
Then I cried for the day by night, and I long'd
    for the night by day.
If I gaz'd at the herons in flight, or paus'd by
    the Tigris' side,
The thought burnt into my soul, ' While you
    watch, an hour has died ; '
And it seem'd that Canopus had wings, and the
    fickle moon and the sun
Were eager to hasten the time when my wretched
    race should be run.

"So I hated my life, yet I shrank from Death,
    till at last in despair,
I humbled my brow in the dust, and pray'd unto
    Allah this prayer :
' O God, if it be that Thou deignest to harken
    when mortals beseech —
' If the Earth be Thine, and the souls therein —
    if Thy power can reach
' To the depth of our need — if pity be Thine —
    I entreat Thee to hear !

'The world was bright, and my bride I lov'd,
 and my friend was dear —
'Was it wrong to delight in Thy gifts? Dost
 Thou bid us Thy bounty despise?
'If Beauty is not to be seen, O Lord, why give
 us these eyes?
'But when Death holds the goblet of life to our
 lips the vintage is sour;
'Beauty and pleasure, and love itself cannot
 charm us an hour
'If we fear they will fade like mirage — that a
 breath may destroy;
'On the eddies of Change and the sands of
 Doubt we can build not our joy.
'Daily I offer'd Thee fivefold thanks, believing
 Thee just,
'Till the hand of my friend was frozen in mine:
 then my hope and my trust
'Were undone, and I said in my impious wrath
 that Allah allows
'Eblis and Death to wanton at will in His earthly
 house,
'While He in Paradise dwelleth apart, contented
 to hear
'The praise which the angels who fell not in sin
 attune to His ear.
'But Lord, if Thou lovest a human soul, and
 wouldst silence the shout
'Of Thine arrogant foes, I implore Thou wilt
 deign to cleanse me from doubt.

'What wonder, what wonder Thy Prophets of
 old to worship were stirr'd,
'Since Thy face uncurtain'd they saw, and Thy
 voice unmuffled they heard ?
'Can we know that their faith had prevail'd were
 it not for Thy miracles' aid ?
'O now is the time, and I am the man for a sign
 to persuade !
'If Thy strength, as our fathers declar'd, be
 supreme, oh show me a sign,
'Shed but a drop of Thy mercy on me, and my
 zeal shall be Thine ;
'Thee as my God I will own, as the Lord of the
 earth and the sky,
'If Thou answer the pray'r I now offer — oh
 grant that I never may die ! '

" So I pray'd like to one full of doubts if there
 be any virtue in pray'r,
And would fledge with the feathers of scorn the
 appeal he shoots in despair.
But sleep made a truce with my grief, and down
 to my bedside came
The Angel of Revelation, with scrolls and a
 sword of flame :
And he opened the scrolls, and spake, ' Behold
 the book of thy fate,
'Where thy deeds were written before thy birth ;
 behold the date
'Appointed for thee to depart — after three-score
 years and one ;

‘On the eve of the fast of Ramadan thy records
　　are done.’

Then I fain had seen whether further bliss to
　　my life was decreed,

But the book was written in heavenly script, which
　　no mortal may read.

And the Angel said, ‘Thy doom was this till
　　thou madest a cry,

‘ For a sign that Allah is Lord ; He grants that
　　thou shalt not die.’

Thus speaking he burnt the scroll of my fate,
　　and I strove to embrace

His knees, for none might bear to look on his
　　radiant face ;

But he vanish’d like music still’d.   In the morn-
　　ing when I awoke

The stone had roll’d from my heart, and my neck
　　had slipp’d its yoke.

“ As when a traveler bound for Fez from his
　　route doth stray,

Where the hot Harmattan blows, and feverish
　　calentures play

In his dizzy brain, and losing hope he wishes to
　　die,

Until from the crest of a billow of sand he can
　　feebly descry

In the hollow beneath a cluster of trees and his
　　caravan,

And he shouts to his friends, and is sav’d ; so the
　　rapture of living ran

Again thro' my soul when I woke that morn
    and saw by my side
My Lily of Shiraz asleep, Leila, my beautiful
    bride !
And I kiss'd her lids, and whisper'd, 'Awake,
    the demon has fled !
'And Love is the Sultan again!' Oh the tears
    of joy she shed!

"Exulting I greeted the sun, and I felt no
    longer the curse
Of being a bubble of Time in a timeless uni-
    verse.
Unsadden'd, I watch'd the Tigris flow and the
    Galaxy shine —
Let them rush on their race forever, the length
    of their race was mine!
Beauty could never outlive me, and joy could
    never exceed
The scope of my life; I could look without
    shame on a moth or a weed.
So the years flew by, but I reck'd not; my life
    had the amplitude
Of the ocean which waits for its streams. Men
    weep over bygone good :
The pleasures that hover'd but once within grasp,
    and unseiz'd flew away,
Had the loveliest plumage ; how dull and com-
    mon the pleasures that stay !
But I was absolv'd from the demon Regret,
    which soundeth a knell

When the goblets clink at the feast of delight,
    and whispers farewell;
That presage of parting that darkens the spirits
    of friends who meet
Cast not its shadow on me — my sweet was a
    permanent sweet.
I leisurely grew to the stature and strength of a
    dignified man,
Who summons not Haste to complete the building
    which Wisdom began,
But layeth his courses with care, and leaveth no
    crevice for Time;
And before I would venture to fly, I patiently
    taught me to climb.
I had wealth enough in my purse, and children
    play'd in my house,
And Suhreh's face had delighted me less than
    the face of my spouse.
I drank of the poet's wine, I tasted the bread of
    the sage;
I fear'd no more lest a hand unseen, ere I fin-
    ish'd the page,
Should close the book; and I smil'd, when my
    neighbors with trembling breath
Lamented that life is brief, and utter'd their hor-
    ror of death.
The rose-trees bloom'd in my garden, my branches
    hung low with fruit;
I serv'd the Khalif as vizier, and mighty was my
    repute.

My vow unto Allah I kept — not a monk of the
    sky-blue frock
More zealously wafted his incense of praise, but
    I seal'd with the lock
Of silence my lips concerning the Angel's visit
    to me
And I dar'd not to whisper to Leila herself of
    that solemn decree.

"So the current of life ran eagerly down from
    the mountainous steep
Which sends youth forth at a passionate speed,
    till, placid and deep,
It flows with the gait of a King thro' the plain
    of our middle years,
And seemeth almost to pause at times, as the
    ocean it nears.
Like a banyan my roots struck far in the earth,
    and my branches wide
Renew'd their strength in the earth again, and
    on every side
Put forth new shoots — from a single seed an
    acre of shade!
And round the knees of the parent my children's
    children play'd.
Then the time approach'd when the Angel an-
    nounc'd I was fated to die ;
Before that doom had been cancel'd. My terror
    return'd, and I
Fell to doubting again whether Allah would hold
    to his pledge or relent.

On the evening which usher'd the Ramadan fast,
    to the housetop I went
And trembling I saw the infant moon sink into
    her cradle of flowers,
And the stars grow bright, and the city asleep.
    Alone, I counted the hours
Whose march was slow as the step of those who
    follow a bier ;
Thus I sat and watch'd in the tomb of Night,
    with my comrade, Fear.
What if Time should halt? — But no ! for I saw
    on a minaret's tip
Aldébaran like a ruby aflame, then leisurely slip
Into the black horizon's bowl, and slowly the
    Pleiades
Dropt like dew from bough to bough of the cin-
    namon-trees.
Then I fix'd my eyes on the East, where the
    beacon of succor should burn :
Still dark ! Not a glimmer of gray ! Not a pe-
    tal of rose to discern !
I strove to sort the crow-black thread from the
    thread that was white —
In vain, for they both were black. Then, sudden,
    a dapple of light,
Faint as the pallor a young swan casts at dusk
    on a stream,
Crept into the sky and a little bedimm'd the
    stars ; then a gleam,
And the rim of the earth was distinct from the
    sky ; the cheeks of the mist

Flutter'd a delicate pink, as a damsel blushes
    when kiss'd ;
Then diaphanous sapphire tinted the East, and
    over the crest
Of the loftiest peak spread the tender hues of
    pearl in the West !
I could count the veins on my hand ; the horizon's
    raven shrouds
Were dyed with purple and hemm'd with gold,
    and anon the clouds
Were changed to a garden of flowers, more gor-
    geous than Shiraz knows —
Tulips of wonderful hues, and heavenly bowers
    of rose !
And now like the gilded dome of a mosque was
    the glow in the East,
And into the Temple of Day ascended the Great
    High Priest,
While the breeze shook incense out, and the song-
    sters jubilee made :
Allah had granted my prayer — I liv'd, and was
    not afraid !

  " For a season or more, like a thirsty man, my
    pleasures I quaff'd.
' Time overlooks the Vizier,' the Khalif remark'd,
    and I laugh'd ;
' Nay, Sire, a tortoise is Time, and we are the
    hares,' I replied ;
' Tho' he seem to delay, ere the goal he will con-
    quer our fleetfoot pride.'

Those were the words on my tongue, but the
    thoughts I kept in my heart
Had an arrogant ring : ' Halîd shall stay, but
    thou shalt depart,
' In spite of thy power, O King ; the servant
    shall bury his lord.'
O man, never dare to exult, for the swift, invis-
    ible sword
Spareth the brow in the dust, but smiteth the
    insolent head !
Leila, the life of my life, fell sick — ere a month
    she was dead.
At her grave with ashes I crown'd me, and wept ;
    then, awful there burst
On my soul a storm of despair which thunder'd,
    Thou, wretch, art accurs'd !
Unrighteous the boon I had ask'd, and Allah had
    granted me life —
But Love, the enricher of all, lay dead in the
    grave of my wife.
Had I pray'd that she might be deathless with
    me, would Allah have heard?
Too late, she was gone, and forever ! *forever* —
    the terrible word,
The whisper sent back from the Past, the echo
    of Fate and Regret,
The warning that unto the strut of our Pride, a
    limit is set !
Not at once could I master its meaning — my
    grief was too stormy for that !

But slowly, as day after day the Sun in his palace sat,
Yet shone not upon her return; and as in the
usual hum
Of familiar household voices, her voice, the sweetest, was dumb;
And as I listen'd at Night for the sound of her
step in my room,
Yet the pitiless silence was never disturb'd —
then I measured my doom!
Think you the world has compassion? It hurried on just as before :
Men went to their toil or their revel, and children
play'd at my door;
The nightingales sang just as sweetly, the rose-
trees blossom'd as red,
As if unaware that my joy had set, that my darling was dead!
And the months on her grave the cyclamen
strew'd and anemones bright —
As if 't were a spot where lovers might come to
take their delight.

"My kindred entreated me kindly at first, and
strove to console,
And the good Khalif us'd to mingle his words of
cheer with my dole.
' Be not dejected, Halîd : thou art wise, and the
Sages have taught
' That the sorrows and fears which beset us on
earth shall vanish — that naught

'Which we suffer below shall endure — that even
      our grief has an end,
'If we hark for the rustle of Azrael's wings, for
      he is our friend,
'And hastens to rescue. Like pilgrims, thro' life
      we wander a while,
'And are lur'd from our path by its beauty; its
      pleasures beguile,
'We will travel no farther; our heaven is here,
      and here we will stop :
'So we tent by the pool of delight, but our thirst
      is unslak'd; and then drop
'The illusions! The world thro' our fingers
      glides, like rain thro' a sieve,
'And nothing abides — all is dream! here no
      absolute pleasure can live !
'So we learn from the eddies and toss of this
      vehement earthly tide
'To hope for a heavenly shore where we shall
      forever abide.
'And we who have journey'd the farthest in life
      stand nearest the gate
'Where infinite joy, and the loves we have lost,
      our coming await.'

" I groan'd at the stab of his comforting words,
      yet I dar'd not reveal
My hideous secret ; no balsam of hope my spirit
      could heal.
But as when a rower refrains from his oars the
      slender caïque

Still glideth ahead, but with lessening speed, so a
    man, when weak
From affliction, by habit performs what erst he
    did by his will;
Joyless I wrought as before, impell'd by life's
    impetus still.
Then the good King died and my friends were
    muffled up one by one,
Like the moon and the stars when over the sky
    a tempest is blown,
And I remain'd in the dark. Woe, woe to the
    desolate sire,
Who lags too long in the seat to which his chil-
    dren aspire!
Their wish they dissembled at first, but I knew
    from their loveless eye
That they chaf'd at my weary delay, and secretly
    hop'd I would die.
Not love, but an irksome duty, directed their con-
    duct to me;
Not a single caress was unreckon'd, no word, no
    courtesy free.
When I spoke they restlessly listen'd, and said
    in contempt, ' What you say
' May once have been wise, but Wisdom has al-
    ter'd its fashion to-day;
' The world is the prize of the young, whose
    motives you cannot know;
' Sit you by the hearth; let us act; we tire of
    your long-ago.'

And sometimes I heard them disputing what age
 a man may attain:
One cited that Noah was the oldest; 'But,' answer'd another, ''t is plain
' The measure we use for the Prophets cannot be
 us'd for us all ;
' In the youth of the world there were giants, but
 men are now puny and small.
'Already Halìd has exceeded the mean ; methinks it is strange,
' That in spite of his burden of years, his countenance showeth no change.'

 " Ah, ready are we to evade the duty we ought
 to endure !
At morn we surmise, and at noon we suspect, and
 by night we are sure !
A hint shall attaint the unspotted when jealousy
 holds the assise,
And evil desire soon finds an excuse that tes-
 tifies.
My kinsfolk threw over deceit ere long. ' We bid
 thee reveal,'
Quoth one, and his features were ice, 'how it
 happens that Time cannot steal
' A jot from the speed of thy life.' Then another, with voice more stern,
' Grievous indeed, at the best, is an old man's
 fretful sojourn :
' But Nature has ruth for his heirs and for him,
 and calls him away.

'What truce hast thou bargain'd with her that
    she grants this weary delay ?'
I was mute, but no doubt had I spoken their an-
    ger had found in my speech,
As it found in my silence, a ready offense to
    blame and impeach.
'Now mark ye, 't is as I suspected,' said one, 'he
    dares not deny
'That a devil possesses his soul — that he has a
    djin for ally!'
'Yea, and yet blacker than that!' cried another,
    'the Prophet declares
'That when Eblis strides forth to his harvest, the
    shape of a mortal he wears ;
'Our sire Halîd went to Heaven long since ; this
    creature we see,
'Disguis'd in his form, is the Devil.' 'Or else,'
    quoth a third, 'it may be
'That the soul of Halîd is ensnarl'd in a secret
    and pardonless crime,
'And Allah ordains for his sin that he be not de-
    liver'd by Time.'
So near struck the guess to the mark that I shud-
    der'd, but still I was mute.
'With merely a word or a look, the innocent
    quickly refute
'The charges that rest not on truth,' the eldest
    then taunted, 'but thou
'Art asham'd to confide in thy sons ; thy guilti-
    ness lowers thy brow.

' Be he wicked or wizard, my brothers, 't is surely
    unlawful to give
' Our shelter to him any longer !   The good with
    the bad should not live,
' For sinful example will subtly envenom the vir-
    tuous heart.
' Our souls we must guard from contagion : to-day
    this man must depart.'
Ah, never is wanting the plea of religion to jus-
    tify wrong !
In vain shall the righteous appeal when a text
    emboldens the strong !
' We do but the will of the Prophet ! ' my chil-
    dren exclaim'd ; ' Away ! '
' Ye follow your wicked desires — I go — but
    the Lord will repay ' —
Flash'd my tongue ere I sheath'd it in silence
    again.   Then my feet
Pass'd over the pitiless threshold ; alone I grop'd
    in the street.

" The Earth lay open before me, but nowhere
    in it a home —
No Mecca, no grave, at the end of my journey !
    Forever to roam,
That was my fate. — Much I pass, too long were
    the anguish to tell ;
To speak of hell's agonies calmly, we first must
    have risen from hell.
Not a road in the East or the West but my san-
    dals have startled its dust :

Not a land but has taught me how bitter and
    hard is an alien's crust,
And how cruel are men to their fellows; the
    weak and poor are the grain
Which the millstones Power and Riches grind,
    unheeding their pain.
If I settled perchance in a village, and sought
    but to follow a trade,
The townsmen would whisper and doubt, and
    then they would harshly upbraid,
And call me a creature unholy, and oust me with
    insults and blows:
For those who are not like the many, the many
    regard as their foes.
I counted no longer the days — Time was nothing
    to me who had all;
They only a calendar need whose pittance of
    seasons is small,
For which a scant measure of glory, or learning,
    or love, may be bought;
But I, with the hoard of the ages to spend, could
    purchase me nought:
A beggar 'mid riches, like him who starves in a
    mine of gold.
Wearily, wearily over my head the indolent cen-
    turies roll'd, —
Ever the brazen sun by day, and by night the
    languid moon;
Nature a dullard that mumbles by rote her mo-
    notonous tune,

And waywardly fondles her playthings, then
    tosses them by, disdain'd ;
Each Spring dismantled by Autumn, no perma-
    nent victory gain'd ;
A circuit of vain preparations! Motionless,
    wearily I
Like the spike of a dial was fix'd, and saw them
    wheel sluggishly by !

"Oh God, how I struggled to break from this
    hideous prison of life !
How my heart leapt up when I heard of a town
    where the plague was rife :
Thither I hurried and tended the sick, but the
    pestilent air
Was as Spring-time balm to my nostrils ; I flour-
    ish'd and Death flourish'd there !
If I plung'd into battle an unseen hand turn'd
    the arrows aside ;
And the deadliest poison refresh'd me like wine.
    Thereafter I tried
The arts forbidden and black of the Magian
    tribe who explore
The innermost bowels of life ; I studied the
    alchemist's lore ;
I grop'd in the sorcerers' caves, — in vain ! They
    are cheats who pretend
To discover the process by which the dust and
    the spirit blend !
We are, but wherefore, or how, that only Allah
    can show :

Think you a wizard His equal, and what He
hideth can know ?
What Allah refuses to Faith we cannot unravel
by Wit :
So I dropt the impossible quest, and learn'd per-
force to submit.

" I watch'd like Simurga the ebb and flow of
the Fate of Man —
Wearisome currents, profitless tides, who know-
eth your plan ?
Nations burst into blossom and fill'd the world
with their scent —
Then a sudden frost or a wind, and they shriv-
ell'd and perish'd forespent.
I knew when I quitted a proud-built town that
when I came back
I should find a forest above it, or sand and the
lizards' track.
In the palace of Jamshyd the Great, I have
heard the jackals howl ;
The bats have made them a perch in his mosque :
the hyaenas prowl
Thro' the courts of mighty Karûn; Palmyra 's a
desert again :
Men build, but the spiders which build not, in-
herit the glory of men.
The creeds are but as simoons, which blow from
the East or the West,
And the nations are rushes which bend, but their
roots unshaken rest :

The wind from Medina has veer'd, and freshens
    from Galilee ;
The blood of the Saracen weakens, the Giaour
    is stronger than he —
But the Frank shall not lord it forever, another
    victor shall rise
To call him ancient, and spurn his faith and his
    wisdom as lies.
For only ALLAH abides! Mohammed, and
    Jesus, and Budh,
Are the names men use to draw near to the
    nameless Infinitude,
And be not destroy'd ; of these they can reason,
    to these they can pray, —
But others diviner shall come, and the worship of
    these shall decay,
Till the Vision approach to the Truth, but That
    men never shall see :
If a man be mistaken for God, ah, what must
    God's majesty be!
I think of the time when Allah shall tire of our
    mortal show,
And winnow the race from the Earth, but leave
    me still here below,
Alone on the whirling ball, unpitied, and
    doom'd unforgiven
To drop forever aghast thro' the wildernesses of
    heaven !

  " O you who live with Death at your beck may
    cherish your life !

There is balm, there is balm for your pain, and
    peace at last for your strife!
Despair should not master the heart of a mortal
    permitted to die —
His grief hath a bourne, he may laugh at the
    threats of disaster, but I
And my pangs are eternal. Behold, the very
    Pyramids there
Have crumbled an inch since I saw them last,
    and the ages shall wear.
Their pride to the floor of the desert, to drift
    about in the wind;
And men shall come to behold them, and never a
    vestige find,
And scholars shall doubt their existence, and
    some shall boldly maintain,
' 'T is only an ancient story, to dazzle posterity's
    brain!'
Yet then — when the stones have wasted, my
    life as to-day will be,
For my agony always begins, and there is no
    Past for me.
Look at that beetle which crawls at our feet —
    ah, he shall have Death —
While I — though a man — can never escape
    from the burden of breath!
The curtain which hangs like a pall in front of
    my hopeless eyes
Shall be lifted for all save me — they shall pass
    into Paradise,

Where the odors of blooming tuba-trees thro' the
　　　gardens steal :
Hassan and Leila are there, and they drink of
　　　the Selsebil :
And no recollection of me perturbs their heav-
　　　enly mirth,
For Heaven would less be Heaven, if the thought
　　　of friends on Earth,
Who suffer still in the flesh, the blissful air could
　　　chill :
So they drink of the fount of Delight, and are
　　　bless'd with the Angel's will.
But I, forgotten of all save Woe, can never
　　　forget ;
When I look behind, 't is Remorse — when I look
　　　before 't is Regret.
The rivets of destiny bind my life to this cliff
　　　forlorn —
I shall never see Leila again ! Oh would I had
　　　never been born ! —
You have heard my terrible fate : when you pray
　　　unto God beware
Lest you ask an unhallowèd boon, and He punish
　　　by granting your prayer ! "

　　As he ceas'd, there pass'd us some boisterous
　　　men, and seeing Halid,
They tapp'd their foreheads, and laugh'd, and
　　　shouted to me, ' Would you heed
' The tale of a crazy beggar ? ' He heard, and
　　　unspeakable woe

Struggled with wrath on his haggard face : then
    he turn'd him to go ;
And ere I could summon him back, or rebuke
    those insolent men,
The tombs had shut him from sight, and I saw
    him never again.

INVOCATION.

YE solemn Prophets, who on Sinai's height
Hear God's command the thunder-volley drown,
Who on imperishable tablets write
The precedents of conscience, and bring down
The heavenly code, which levels king and clown :

Dear Poets, who e'er keep the eyes of youth,
Whose souls are as a perfect violin
Melodious, when Beauty plays, or Truth,
Whose genial hearts are hostelries wherein
Courtesy greets all travelers, save Sin ;

Redeemers of humanity, who feel
Vicarious passion, hallowing the scope
Of homely duties ; wizards who reveal
The preciousness of common things, and ope
With wand benign the hidden gates of hope ;

Rapt dreamers of the transcendental dreams
Which are reality ; foretellers of
Perfection which across the future gleams

To dim the present good wherein we move ;
Spokesmen of Freedom, oracles of Love : —

Be my companions, ye that are my kin !
Impeach my doubting heart, my sluggish will !
I hear your call above the cheerless din
Of court and pulpit, senate-house and mill :
O guide my footsteps to your sacred hill !

THE MODERN ODYSSEY.

WILL you follow me thro' space ?
Mount a star-beam, join the race,
Loose the nerve-twin'd cord of sense,
Drop the carnal wrappage, dense ;
Fancy shall our pilot be,
Cosmical, surprising, free !
Quibbling Reason, be thou still, —
Put to us no questions chill ;
While thou panting lagg'st behind
In a logic-net confin'd,
Frolic Fancy at a bound
Truth unperishing hath found !

Quick, bestride the lucent steed !
Time we shall no longer need ;
Day and darkness one appear
When the mighty suns are near.
Earthly measures, bounds, forget,
Let no finite memory fret ;

Pluck away the dread of death —
Fancy hangs not on a breath.

Ready ! Up ! Farewell ! — But slow
At beginning let us go,
Else the earth would dart from sight
Like a cinder in the night.
Watch the plains and mountains shrink :
Yonder straggling blotch of ink
Is a city ; millions thrive
In that brick and granite hive ;
Dwindled to a speck, a spot,
Trifle — now we see thee not !
Higher still ! that tiny cloud
Veils a nation vast and proud ;
Each wee mortal creeping there
Deems his home the nook most fair
Of the universe — nay, more,
Counts himself the world before ;
Everything was made for him,
God exists to please his whim.

Earth now shrivels to a ball,
Shadows o'er its surface fall
Marking where the moon-drawn sea
From the continents is free.
Up ! but yet a moment turn
Just to note where drifts astern
On the ether's billows dull
Luna's gibbous, pitted skull.

See where burning fiercely blue
Sun uplifts his disk to view;
Mottled like chameleon's back,
Now 't is bright, and now 't is black;
Heat he spurts in flaming plumes,
Or in hissing pools consumes,
While he greedily devours
Pelting meteoric showers.

As the phosphorescent wake
Vessels on the ocean make
Spreads, and gleams, and goes astray,
So, above, the Milky Way
Eddies and meanders far —
Every glistening drop a star!
We its broadest flood will swim
Where from here it looks most slim.

Mark how, like a sky of flame,
Mighty Sirius hurls his frame!
He the nearest hapless orbs,
As the sea the rain, absorbs;
Zenith scorches in his flight,
Nadir quivers molten white,
Whirlwinds shriek behind his path
Louder than Hell's fabled wrath.
Whither, monster, dost thou wend?
Waits thy course at last an end?
Wherefore thro' the black abyss
Must thou headlong plunge and hiss?
Do thy wildernesses burn
And no compensation earn?

Guess we cannot, wonder vast!
But should'st thou plunge trebly fast,
Little man's untrammel'd mind
Instantly would leave behind
Thy huge bulk, or he would stay
Thine expanse to mete and weigh.
Thou, chief tyrant of the sky,
Thou art slave to man's small eye!

Here is silence so intense
That the softest whisper hence
Fluttering down the vast inane —
Like hay-fragrance after rain —
Myriad leagues would penetrate
And expand in circles great,
'Till the last vibration tir'd
And in far-off space expir'd.

Force conflicting tugs and rides
Every atom on all sides :
Thro' each mote, as 't were a glass,
Rays from stars uncounted pass;
Yet no jar, no clash destroys
Every atom's perfect poise.

If we hurried tow'rds the West,
Or if Eastward pauseless press'd,
Never should we meet a sign
Of a limit or a line :
When we reach'd the farthest sun
Fancy wots of, but begun

We should find a farther flight
With fresh wonders to delight.

Could we stop that sheaf of rays
Hast'ning tirelessly thro' space,
And their message clearly read
We should be amaz'd indeed!
For those javelins of light
From the Earth began their flight
When the perfect man, the Christ,
On the Cross was sacrific'd.

In mysterious fashion, how
Is the Past the Present now!
How make opposites agree?
How adjust disparity?
How the thought of finite blend
With the infinite no-end?
How shall Fancy reunite
Rest and motion, dark and light?
Contradictions interwed,
And impossible, instead,
Plainly possible appears,
Tho' no wit the problem clears.

Now our cheeks are softly kiss'd
By a drench of stellar mist!
Peradventure, ages hence
It may live in nerve and sense,
When the cosmic wizard, Heat,
Shall ensphere, compact, complete.

Will, then, other Hamlets there
Love, procrastinate, despair?
And will women weep to know
Unrequited passion's woe?
Will another man-like race
Godward, trembling, turn its face,
Crush'd by Circumstance and Time
Slowly, zig-zag, upward climb,
Often asking, as on Earth,
If the prize the pain be worth,
Often halting to inquire,
Wherefore sweat to struggle higher?
But as ages circle round,
Still on loftier plane be found?

Wherefore now with anxious eye
Do you search the star-sown sky?
Homesick for your native hearth,
Do you peer so soon for Earth?
Brush the shadow from your mind —
Little Earth we left behind
Uncomputed time ago;
Where she is we cannot know.
Let the tiny plaything spin
Like a top, her orbit in,
Till perhaps some later day
She again dance in our way.
We still grander worlds to view
Bravely will our flight pursue,
Certain that, where'er we roam,
We shall never leave our home.

LOVE'S DREAD.

Eyes, but for you I had not seen
Her motion, grace, and lovely mien!

Ears, but for you I had not heard
Her voice that spake no loveless word!

And Touch, thou mad'st me understand
Her lips' delight, her soothing hand!

I thank ye for each message brought,
I thank ye for each beauty taught;

But oh, for senses trustier
To give me true reports of her,

Till I might rise myself above
And adequately know my Love!

O careless Fate, love's all to trust
To these frail gossips of the dust!

THE LAST HUNT.

Oh, it 's twenty gallant gentlemen
    Rode out to hunt the deer,
With mirth upon the silver horn
    And gleam upon the spear;

They gallop'd thro' the meadow-grass,
  They sought the forest's gloom,
And loudest rang Sir Morven's laugh,
  And lightest tost his plume.
      There 's no delight by day or night
        Like hunting in the morn;
      So busk ye, gallant gentlemen,
        And sound the silver horn!

They rode into the dark greenwood
  By ferny dell and glade,
And now and then upon their cloaks
  The yellow sunshine play'd;
They heard the timid forest-birds
  Break off amid their glee,
They saw the startled leveret,
  But not a stag did see.
      Wind, wind the horn, on summer morn!
        Tho' ne'er a buck appear,
      There 's health for horse and gentleman
        A-hunting of the deer!

They panted up Ben Lomond's side
  Where thick the leafage grew,
And when they bent the branches back
  The sunbeams darted through;
Sir Morven in his saddle turn'd,
  And to his comrades spake,
"Now quiet! we shall find a stag
  Beside the Brownies' Lake."

Then sound not on the bugle-horn,
 Bend bush and do not break,
Lest ye should start the timid hart
 A-drinking at the lake.

Now they have reach'd the Brownies' Lake —
 A blue eye in the wood —
And on its brink a moment's space
 All motionless they stood :
When, suddenly, the silence broke
 With fifty bowstrings' twang,
And hurtling thro' the drowsy air
 Full fifty arrows sang.
   Ah, better for those gentlemen,
    Than horn and slender spear,
   Were morion and buckler true,
    A-hunting of the deer.

Not one of that brave company
 Shall hunt the deer again ;
Some fell beside the Brownies' Pool,
 Some dropt in dell or glen ;
An arrow pierc'd Sir Morven's breast,
 His horse plung'd in the lake,
And swimming to the farther bank
 He left a bloody wake.
   Ah, what avails the silver horn,
    And what the slender spear ?
   There 's other quarry in the wood
    Beside the fallow deer !

O'er ridge and hollow sped the horse
  Besprent with blood and foam,
Nor slacken'd pace until at eve
  He brought his master home.
How tenderly the Lady Ruth
  The cruel dart withdrew !
" False Tirrell shot the bolt," she said,
  " That my Sir Morven slew ! "
     Deep in the forest lurks the foe,
      While gaily shines the morn ;
     Hang up the broken spear, and blow
     A dirge upon the horn.

MAN IN NATURE.

CLIMBING up the hillside beneath the summer
    stars
  I listen to the murmur of the drowsy ebbing
    sea ;
The newly-risen moon has loos'd her silver zone
  On the undulating waters where the ships are
    sailing free.

O moon, and O stars, and O drowsy summer sea
  Drawing thy tide from the city up the bay,
I know how you will look and what your bounds
    must be,
  When we and our sons have forever pass'd
    away.

You shall not change, but a nobler race of men
  Shall walk beneath the stars and wander by
      the shore ;
I cannot guess their glory, but I think the sky
    and sea
  Will bring to them more gladness than they
      brought to us of yore.

ECHOES FROM THE GARDEN.

1. PRELUDE.

THE Persian Muses of the glowing heart
Dwelt not on Heliconian heights apart,
Midway 'twixt gods and men, but friendly came
Down to our Earth, as trustful and as tame
As birds that sing and build their nests on boughs
Which almost sweep the windows of a house:
They, who might wander Heaven with seraphim,
Stoop'd to the haunts of Man, and walk'd with
    him
Along the footpaths of mortality, nor fear'd
Lest, better known, they might be less rever'd.
They trusted, for they lov'd : their home they
    chose
The Garden of Mosella, where the rose
Spreads gorgeous branches, and the bulbul sings,
And butterflies wear jewels on their wings,
And where the cadent drippings of a rill
The intervals of silence sweetly fill.

There Hafiz sang, and Saadi moraliz'd,
While many listen'd, spell-bound and surpris'd ;
For one address'd the mind, and one the heart,
And both were masters of the poet's art.
These and Firdausi are the matchless three
To honor whom the Persians all agree :
Him of the Kingly Epic they revere,
Saadi they trust their lives aright to steer,
But, to a heart, they love their Hafiz best,
Who liv'd when Laura's lover charm'd the West.
We all have heard Petrarca, and we know
His exquisite abandonment to woe,
His love, not greater than his verse could bear,
His lyric sighs, his rhythmical despair ;
But we have not heard Hafiz, who has sung
To centuries of lovers.   Old and young,
Thro' days of peace and grim foreboding times
Persians have kindled to his magic rhymes,
And, oft as Love has fir'd a Persian youth,
Two hearts have felt that Hafiz spake the truth.

Joy ! joy ! no past, no clime hath Poesie !
The love she utters dies not, nor can she !
To-day, o'er seas and centuries I hear
The murmur of a lute, the laughter clear
Of revelers unwearied, and there floats
The breath of many flowers with the notes,
And glasses tinkle when the music ends, —
'T is Hafiz in the Garden, with his friends.

2. LOVE, THE BUILDER.

Strew roses, and jessamines scatter,
    And into our cup pour wine ;
The roof of the sky we will shatter,
    And build us a dwelling divine !

As high as our hopes we will build it,
    Desire shall hew us the beams,
The sun of contentment shall gild it,
    The walls shall be painted with dreams.

We 'll make captive the beauty of May-time,
    Not a leaf of its blossoms shall fade !
Our time shall forever be playtime,
    The flight of our youth shall be stay'd.

We will leave not a corner for sighing,
    No wish shall be broken in twain,
We will silence all whispers of dying,
    There shall never be any more pain.

We shall always be strangers to sorrow ;
    The flames on our shrine of delight
Shall glow at our waking to-morrow
    As they glow at our kisses to-night.

Then kiss, and our home is completed,
    Ev'ry wish to fulfilment shall haste,
And the sweetness of pleasures repeated
    Forever the sweetest shall taste.

3. THE CONSTANT LOVER.

Suleika's were the rosy lips,
  And Zeyneb's were the lustrous eyes,
And Fatima more sweetly sang
  Than nightingales in Paradise.
Zobayda — she was shining tresses,
And Leila — she was dove-caresses,
  Dove and serpent, love and lies.

Amîma had — but I forget
  If she was fair, or simply true ;
Suleima's kisses were the best
  Till I Zarîfa's kisses knew, —
Zarîfa, maid of tears and laughter,
Swift summer clouds and sunshine after,
  Tears and kisses sweet as dew.

O roses, roses of my youth,
  I wonder are ye wither'd now?
Nay, be not jealous of those buds,
  Shirîn, my soul's sultana thou !
For they were but a May-day pleasure,
While thou art my eternal treasure —
  All my love to thee I vow !

4. POSTPONE NOT PLEASURE.

Prevent me not ! who knows, who knows
How soon the petals of the rose
  Must fade and drop ?

Forbid me not the ruby wine,
Deny me not the kiss divine, —
Who knows how soon thy lips, or mine,
A little clod of dust will close,
    And pleasure stop?

In Spring, we 'll have the joy of Spring —
Kisses and wine and caroling —
    The blithe are wise.
When April comes another year
Can'st promise he will find me here?
To-day is ours — no more is clear;
The joy that has the brightest wing
    The swiftest flies!

5. THE INVITATION.

Be my messenger, wind of the West!
    Into my Lady's lattice blow,
Kiss for me her lips and her breast —
    Whose the kisses are, she will know.

Shed upon her the roses' scent —
    Breath of roses asleep at dusk —
Waft the nightingale's love-lament,
    Carry the odors of lily and musk!

Fan the flame of her heart's desire,
    Bind thy swiftness under her feet;
Tell her, I see the glow-worm's fire,
    Tell her, the night for lovers is fleet.

Go, my messenger, out of the West,
　Her chamber-lattice is open to thee ;
Kiss, O kiss her lips and her breast, —
　She will arise and hasten to me !

6. THE APOLOGY OF HAFIZ.

Nay, dervish of the hollow cheek,
　Have charity, and do not scold :
Tho' you be strong, and I be weak,
　The ways to heaven are manifold.

The rut your pious feet have worn
　Upon the flagg'd monastic floor,
The self-inflicted scourges borne,
　The beads repeated o'er and o'er,

The dust you sprinkle on your head,
　The prayers, the fasts — all these but show
'T is roundabout the road you tread
　By which to Paradise to go.

Let him who would a dervish be
　His conduct to your care confide,
But can you steer my ship for me
　On waters you have never tried ?

Where roses bloom I say my prayer,
　My monastery is an inn,
My brother-monks no sackcloth wear,
　No fasting pales their ruddy skin.

A damsel, whose narcissus lips
    E'en you would guess were meant to kiss,
Smiling across the carpet trips
    And brims our cups with liquid bliss.

Then stories interspers'd with song —
    Than merry song what holier hymn ?
And laughter runs like rills along,
    Till twilight makes the tavern dim.

A parting quaff, a gay goodnight,
    And then each comrade homeward wends,
Beneath the stars' mysterious light,
    And feels the nobler for his friends.

" A jovial life 's a life of sin," —
    I 've heard your precepts all before ;
" The Devil follows pleasure in,
    Tho' but a crack you ope the door."

You may be right — and yet, and yet,
    Suppose that when we come to die
Our Lord inquire what joys we met
    In Earth, *His Earth*, would you reply ? —

" O Lord, who art a jealous God,
    I cannot answer Thy demand ;
The straight and narrow road I trod,
    And never peep'd to either hand.

" My bed a stone, my raiment sack,
    My dwelling-place a gloomy cell,

O let the scars upon my back
  My tale of self-denial tell!

" I shunn'd the vulgar, godless crew,
    Lest their contagion harm my soul;
  No other wish on Earth I knew
    Than to be freed from Earth's control;

" No joy's postponement did I grudge,
    No pious hardship, night or day;
  For well I knew that Thou, O judge,
    Most bountifully wilt repay.

" My sins, my many sins, I fought;
    My ill desires I mortified;
  My soul no earthy taint has brought, —
    Unless it be a blur of pride

" To glory that I am of those,
    The few, who Thy commands enjoy,
  And never palter'd with Thy foes,
    Whom Thou shalt utterly destroy."

  This, dervish, of your mortal task
    Most truly could you testify;
  But if the Lord my deeds should ask,
    I must in honesty reply:

" Dear God of friendship, love, and grace,
    Ere I had wander'd far on Earth,
  It seem'd so lovable a place
    I could but thank thee for my birth.

" I soon discern'd that good and bad,
  Delight and grief were intertwin'd,
But deem'd it righteous to be glad,
  And suffer'd not a peevish mind.

" I could not think that Thou hadst set
  Pure joys our spirits to ensnare ;
Thou art no fowler with a net,
  To take Thy creatures unaware.

" And so when pleasure beckon'd me
  I dreaded no unseen decoy ;
I held that they best worship Thee
  Who drink the deepest of Thy joy.

" O lovely hast Thou made our world, —
  By day, a garden of surprise,
By night, the firmament unfurl'd ;
  I dwelt, methought, in Paradise.

" And what divine companions there !
  I saw in every fellow-man
Some mark of Thy creative care,
  Thy pattern round each vessel ran.

" No fast I kept, my prayers I miss'd,
  No weary pilgrimage I took,
But oft the rosiest lips I kiss'd,
  And lov'd Thy holy, living Book.

" I did not fret nor speculate
  Concerning dooms of blest or curst,

Nor drew me charts of heaven's estate,
　But wish'd to roam the earthly, first.

" And nothing made my trust so deep
　In the fair issue of thy plan
As that Thou deemest Earth too cheap
　For the eternal home of man.

" Its love, its splendor, its delight,
　Its beauty always at the brim,
Forever might content his sight
　Hadst Thou not higher bliss for him.

" I took Thy gifts with thankful heart,
　And if few thoughts of heaven I had,
It was because I knew Thou art
　On Earth with us, when we are glad."

This, dervish, this shall be my plea,
　Or good or bad, the Judge will show ;
Your heaven could ne'er be heaven to me,
　My heaven on Earth you will not know.

7. THE POET AND FAME.

Sweetheart, you flatter when you say
　" Immortal Hafiz ! "　Tell the truth,
My beard already turneth grey, —
　Immortals never lose their youth.

The poet dies, his songs remain
　An age or two, for men's delight ;

When mine they sing, I live again :
How short the bow — how long the flight !

8. THE SECRET OF HAFIZ.

I have heard a fearful secret :
To the Shah I will not tell it,
I will hide it from my sweetheart,
From my merry, dear companions,
    When they ask.

This it is : The clod I trample
Was the skull of Alexander,
And the waters of the ocean
In the veins of mighty princes
    Once ran red.

And the dust-clouds of the desert
Were the lips of lovely women :
Where are they, and they who kiss'd them ?
Power dies, and beauty passes,
    Nought abides.

Where is Jamshyd, and his beaker ?
Solomon, and where his mirror ?
Which of all the wise professors
Knows when Kaus and Jamshyd flourish'd ?
    Who can tell ?

They were mighty, yet they vanish'd ;
Names are all they left behind them ;

Glory first, and then an echo, —
Then the very echo hushes,
    All is still.

O my Shah, ask not my secret!
Sweetheart, I must hide it from you!
They who hear it are not merry:
Power dies, and beauty passes,
    Nought abides.

DISENCHANTMENT.

SOLILOQUY OF VICTOR FAUVEL, NATURALIST.

So Love's but an April fashion,
    And Hope the caprice of young years?
Then enough of the cheats of passion,
    I am tir'd of laughter and tears;
I am tir'd of profitless changes,
    Which the callow seek with zest;
The suspicion of fraud estranges
    Delight from the doubting breast.

Once, Nature was tenderly subtle;
    Dissembling her soulless plan,
She granted each impotent shuttle
    To deem itself free, and a man:
He perceiv'd not the fingers fatal
    That toss'd him along the loom;
She whisper'd of lives prenatal
    And of love out-soaring the tomb.

She flatter'd, as flatters a woman
　　To curtain the waning of love :
" I have dower'd thee, darling, tho' human,
　　With gifts of the gods above :
When the Earth was at its beginning
　　I foresaw thy glory a-wing,
And I patiently waited, spinning
　　Robes meet for creation's King.

" I fashion'd for thee each wonder,
　　I varied the seasons' flight,
Kept day and darkness asunder,
　　Strew'd bloom on the paths of blight :
The sky and the earth and the ocean
　　Are thine, and their broods are thine ;
For the world but reveals the devotion
　　I feel for thee, Lover divine ! "

Ah, flattery deftly season'd
　　Is sweeter than truth to the ear ;
Mankind would never have reason'd,
　　If Nature had been sincere ;
We had dream'd thro' our haughty vision,
　　Beguil'd to the end of the show,
But — worse than her wrath or derision —
　　She dotes, and allows us to know.

As a child that is sated with playing,
　　When slumber upon him falls,
Forgets the tale he was saying
　　To his toys, and spurns his dolls,

So Nature grows weary of feigning;
　What odds if her puppets see
They are only puppets?　Complaining
　Cannot render them men, and free.

Has she wax'd, then, suddenly spiteful
　Tow'rds the innocents she creates?
Ah no, yet the truth is frightful —
　She neither loves us, nor hates:
Impassive, she watches each bubble,
　Let it hover, or let it burst;
The corn is to her as the stubble.
　She breedeth the best and the worst.

We awake from her spell narcotic
　To the knowledge of Earth and Hell;
Ah, why should a Power despotic
　Begrudge us to lengthen the spell?
'T were as easy with sensuous fancies
　To soothe us and entertain,
As to conjure up devilish dances,
　And to open the sluices of pain.

Farewell to the rapture of kisses,
　Farewell to the hope in the bud,
If we guess that our holiest bliss is
　But a trick of the ripening blood!
That, that is the foulest of treasons,
　To make passion itself a decoy:
Ah, night and day and the seasons
　Can never again bring joy!

We know : and the pangs of perdition
   Begin with our knowledge to ache ;
Our Eden is lost thro' suspicion,
   As the first thro' the wile of the snake ;
Fresh lips have a savor of ashes,
   And in young eyes Death peers through,
And the voice of the Preacher clashes,
   As we vow our vows most true.

Spare wrath, 't is begotten of folly,
   And barren is windy regret ;
There will never grow poppy nor moly
   Whose juices might help us forget ;
The sane heads bow in submission,
   While the mad and the bad rebel ;
To be wise is to know our condition,
   Unbias'd by Heaven or Hell.

So the wise intelligence deeper
  ' Sifts the real from the things that seem,
And is conscious, as is the sleeper
   Who dreams that he dreams a dream,
That he is the deed and the doer,
   The skiff and the mastering tide,
Now victim and now pursuer,
   Self-hostile and self-allied.

Not in arrogance, lacking a title,
   Do I speak for our cheated race ;
I have labor'd without requital,
   I have felt despair's embrace,

I have been as a drum for dirges
   And a pipe for the lips of mirth,
I have wielded a penitent's scourges,
   I have hop'd in the glory of Earth!

I have known young love's caresses,
   And the passion of lip and eye,
And the kiss that curses or blesses,
   And a magical earth and sky, —
When to hint of changes were treason,
   And to utter a doubt were crime,
When the body and soul and reason
   Seem'd loos'd from the tethers of time.

Last year, what were honors and learning?
   All pages were lit with one name, —
One glance set my spirit yearning, —
   One whisper was sweeter than fame!
I vow'd that our love was eternal,
   My joy was to hear her command, —
Had she pointed to perils infernal,
   I had willingly follow'd her hand!

Now, her countenance cannot awaken
   One chord in my bosom to play,
For the seasons have stealthily taken
   Our mutual passion away:
'T was no quarrel that clove us asunder,
   No loveless nor petulant word;
We meet without tremor, and wonder
   How either could e'er have been stirr'd.

As a fisherman listlessly gazes
   In a pool that is clear and profound,
And beholds, 'mongst the nethermost mazes,
   The face of a maiden long drown'd,
And at sight of her tranquil beneath, he
   Is startled to pity and dread, —
So thro' the dim waters of Lethe
   I look on my love that is dead.

I have said, when a thrall unto sorrow,
   Love slackens, but grief holds fast ;
And behold, as I spoke, ere the morrow,
   I smil'd, and my grief was past ;
Then I thought, hate cannot be banish'd,
   I swore that remorse would remain, —
Each sway'd me a moment, and vanish'd
   Like a gust over standing grain.

So I noted how Nature impinges
   At all points upon the quick,
Making life either tickles or twinges,
   As our tissues are healthy or sick ;
We are only the slaves of emotion,
   Tho' we brave it in freemen's form ;
Fond mariners toss'd on the ocean,
   To fancy that we are the storm !

Ah, bitter is truth, first tasted,
   And knowledge hath nettles, like sin !
I reckon the long years wasted,
   And I cannot smother chagrin ;

For I too, like the feeble and fickle,
  Have been lur'd from my purpose away, —
A worldling for Nature to tickle,
  A harp for Emotion to play.

Much passes, much glory and glamor,
  As I penetrate Life's disguise,
And, surveying our pitiful drama
  With sober, uncheated eyes,
See that Instinct, protean deceiver,
  Under moraller epithets reigns,
And that Love 's but a vernal fever, —
  Much passes, yet something remains.

Call it fortitude, call it defiance,
  Or scorn for the frauds of the pulse,
A fortitude nourish'd by Science
  That neither desponds nor exults ;
But measures its dungeon coldly,
  And dares to cross-question its doom,
Computes life's eclipses, and boldly
  Would shatter the lid of the tomb.

Unconscious the world and its warder,
  Yet a conscious mortal them views ;
Tho' he be but the puppet of Order,
  Still he chooses, or seemeth to choose ;
'T is a paradox ? Well, let us scan it,
  Tho' never shall we understand ;
And knowledge to build on is granite,
  But emotion is shifting sand.

Let Love still hector his minions,
    Let dupes, if they must, aspire,
I will furl my ambition's pinions,
    And deaden the nerves of desire;
I will pitch me a tent of quiet
    And therein with my mind sojourn;
Afar from men's folly and riot,
    I will learn what a man may learn.

Give me facts — not the pallor nor blushes
    Of passion's chameleon cheeks;
Ere a merciless destiny crushes,
    I will hearken what Science speaks.
Let me cease, then, from tears and from laughter,
    Delusions and sham and show!
Grant me reason now, rest hereafter, —
    I ask not to feel, but to know!

WAVERLEY REVISITED.

RETROSPECT AND OUTLOOK.

Up from the waters of life, up from invisible
    sources,
    Spring, — the Youth of the Year, Spring, —
        the blithe and divine,
Like the fresh, salt air of the sea, reviver of
    virginal forces,
    Breathes on this Waverley land, long ago
        homestead of mine.
Maple and cedar rejoice, the orchard of apple-
    trees blushes,

By her ineffable kiss kindled with love and
    delight :
Robert-o'-Lincoln has come, the cat-birds call,
    and the thrushes
Garland their thickets with song from the day-
    break into the night.

Spring-time in Italy — oh, the indescribable
    splendor !
Florence, the Lily, afloat in an ocean of quiver-
    ing green ;
Fragrance of lemon and thyme, and rustle of
    cypresses slender
Stirr'd by the breezes which waft the carol of
    throstles unseen !
Mystical unison, blending of strength and splen-
    dor and sweetness,
Pageant of noonday enhanc'd when moon-
    beams hallow the night —
Love interfusing the soul with visions of joy and
    completeness —
This is the magic of Italy's Spring — the
    spell, the delight !

Spring-time at Athens — a chrism of hues from
    ethereal fountains !
Shimmer of tremulous waves, amethyst wed-
    ding with gold,
Emeralds set in the purple of immemorial moun-
    tains,
Veils of violet, opaline mists o'er the horizon
    unroll'd !

Whithersoever she wanders, Spring on her beautiful mission
Touches with rapture the sky, wakens to
laughter the Earth;
But we remember as fairest of all her first ap-
parition,
When her miraculous wand transfigur'd the
place of our birth.

Spirit of infinite Youth, thou modest yet masterful Power —
Quick'ning ephemeral weeds and the heart of
the secular oak,
Knowing the longings of man, and the needs of
the bee and the flower,
Maid of the radiant face, maid of the violet
cloak, —
Stubble and furrows of death, and desolate
branches and sadness
Winter bequeaths unto thee, and lo! at a sign,
at a word,
Earth is a garden again, the world is a quire of
gladness,
Meadows and forests are gay, and every tree
has a bird!

Nature, the tender and strong, the dear inex-
haustible mother,
Having no Past to regret, suffers no loss or
decay;

Bloodroot and arbutus up she calls from the
leaves which smother,
Deep in the seed that she drops buries the
promise of May.
Seasons revolve and depart, but the Springtide
forever returning
Setteth the pulses a-dance in the veins of the
indolent year,
Into the rubble and mould she breathes an indis-
tinct yearning,
Opening eyes, thro' the bourgeoning twigs and
clover to peer.

Lilac-tufts nodding at me, wistaria flaunting thy
blossom,
Happy again and careless are ye, triumphant
and proud!
Twenty and over you count the throbbings of
Youth in your bosom —
Unto the year of our life only one Spring is
allow'd!
Now as I visit again the unforgettable places,
Here is the glorious Spring and the bygone
pageant I knew,
Jubilant Youth as of old disports and the land-
scape embraces,
But ah! no longer the eyes of a child look out
on the view!

There is the staunch-built house — but I'll cross
not its threshold enchanted;

Strangers, I know, are within, unaware that
　　they dwell in a tomb ;
How can they slumber and toil and laugh in a
　　sepulchre haunted ?
Ghosts if I enter'd would rise to greet me in
　　every room.
So I will turn from the house where vernal re-
　　nascence avails not —
Relic of joys that are fled and of vanishing
　　mortals, it stands —
Turn to behold once again and marvel at beauty
　　that fails not,
Spring, the Youth of the Year, refreshing
　　these Waverley lands.

Simple indeed is the landscape ! yet haughtily
　　Nature doth love it,
Bidding the emulous months each with a gem
　　to adorn ;
Night after night she unveils the great constella-
　　tions above it,
Day after day she despatches the sun to arouse
　　it at morn.
Only a furlong of meadow, and undulant hil-
　　locks surrounding,
Shaded by clusters of elm, girdled by walnut
　　and oak ;
Glimpses to westward of eve, thro' rifts in the
　　foliage bounding ;
Farther beyond a village unseen, but guess'd
　　from its smoke.

Simple and narrow the landscape looks to my
    soberer vision,   .
   But it was wonderful once, a limitless world
     to the boy,
Ample enough to enframe my pictures of mead-
     ows elysian,
   Learned enough to impart the wisdom of Sor-
     row and Joy !
Here was my earliest school, and Nature, my
     earliest teacher,
   Cunningly told me her lore, pretending to coax
     me to play ;
How she confounded the intricate arts of pedant
     and preacher,
   Arguing never, but on her works stamping
     her *yea* and her *nay !*

Slender and sinuous brook, art gossiping still to
     thy gravel ?
   Formerly Tiber I saw, or Thames in thy hur-
     rying foam ;
Many the paper-built boats I launch'd on thy cur-
     rents to travel,
   "Paris " the willow I call'd, and play'd that
     the boulder was Rome.
Hill to whose top the old lords of the land, the
     pines, have retreated,
   Waiting the final assault, how art thou shrunken
     so low?
Thou wert my Apennines once, thee as my
     Andes I greeted,

When the Decembers of yore mantled thy
  shoulders with snow.

This is the grove where we gather'd the nuts,
  and hither I wander'd,
    Dreaming the dreams of a boy, fervent, fan-
    tastic, and grand ;
Nothing impossible seem'd, nothing unreal, as I
  ponder'd
    Deeds that should draw to my feet the world
    with its laurel in hand.
This was my Kingdom of Fable, and I, the monarch of Fancies,
    Peopled each sylvan retreat with goddesses,
    heroes, and elves ;
Here I commun'd with the souls who blazón the
  deathless romances,
    Talked with historical chiefs, felt I was one of
    themselves.

Innocent glamour of childhood ! halos of beauty
  and wonder
    Circle the tiniest flower, hallow the commonest
    thing ;
Nature has nothing profane, she utters no false-
  hood nor blunder —
    For ev'ry child is a poet, men are all poets in
    Spring !
Memory, is it thy trick, thou cunningly soothing
  magician ?
    Turning to gold the alloy of the Past, annul-
    ling the pain,

Mellowing shadows and lights with the art of the
    master Venetian,
  Stilling the tempests of grief, making the diffi-
    cult plain ?

Would I go back to the cradle, life unimprov'd
    to retravel ?
  Plunge into pitfalls again, rally, endeavor, and
    miss ?
Feel while I grasp'd it the cord which bound me
    to duty unravel ?
  Barter the pangs of a year for the hope, unful-
    fill'd, of a kiss ?
See, as I saw, not the Earth but a wilderness
    newly arisen ?
  Morning and night to beseech the grim, imper-
    turbable sky ?
Weep like an orphan bereft ? like criminal shack-
    led in prison,
  Murmur my impotent prayers to the gods that
    would not reply ?

Shudder again on the brink of murky abysses of
    terror,
  Hearing sardonical laughter rise out of chaos
    below ?
Constantly seek for the truth, yet constantly
    lapse into error ?
  Learn at the end that our knowledge proves
    that we never can know ?

Who would return to the day when evil in men
    he discover'd,
  Horrified saw in his heart seeds of all possible
    crime ?
When o'er his spirit the bat-like imps of iniquity
    hover'd,
  Hinting suspicion of virtue, mocking the fair
    and sublime ?

Stand at a bedside again to watch a beloved one
    fading
  Into the mystery, into the silence — unable to
    save,
Water of Lethe bedewing the lips and the fore-
    head invading ? —
  No, I will turn, I will turn from the Past, for
    the Past is a grave !
Memory, cunning art thou to pluck out the thorns
    of affliction,
  Coyly thou bringest a rose as mark of a funeral
    year !
" Oh, we were happy in childhood ! " that is ma-
    turity's fiction ;
  Let us give thanks that we are not compell'd
    to retrace our career.

Life is a zig-zag at best ; how slowly we strip off
    illusion,
  Dissipate legends and banish the mists that
    befog and confine ;

Neither the Future unborn nor the Past with its
    mould and confusion —
   Only the Present is real, the Present alone is
     divine !
Truth and Reality burn with fulness of light that
    the boldest
   May not endure unprepar'd ; films of delusion
     are spun
Over the splendor which blinds; tho' dimly at
    first thou beholdest,
   When thou shalt need not the clouds, thou shalt
     envisage the sun !

So, should I perish to-day, depart with Spring's
    glory around me,
   Nothing beyond — not a gleam — ere I merg'd
     in unthinkable death,
Here at the home of my youth, where life's ex-
    altation first found me,
   Here would I gird me and say to the Powers
     that granted me breath :
" When you created us men, O Powers almighty,
    immortal,
   Did you intend that this Earth should suffice
     to appease our desire ?
Ah, not a path we can take but leads to your
    heavenly portal,
   Never a stone but it whispers of you, and bids
     us aspire !

" We from the transient and false have sifted
    the true and abiding,
  Piercing the shows of the sense, we find your
    inflexible law ;
Even of you, your majestic mien from our scru-
    tiny hiding,
  We have divin'd the ineffable glory and wis-
    dom and awe.
Twain are the natures in man ; one, selfishly
    headstrong and bestial,
  Tempts him to squander his arrowy years in
    revels and lust ;
But by the other is he reminded of kinship celes-
    tial,
  Bidden to strive for the thoughts that are pure,
    the deeds that are just.

" Strong are the lures of the flesh, magnetic and
    subtle its pleading —
  ' Drink, for the night is at hand ! Kiss, ere
    the lips become clay !
Pleasures rejected will never return, then grasp
    them, unheeding
  Babblers of living hereafter — have we less
    knowledge than they ? '
Self is a crafty attorney, plausible, urgent, and
    clever !
  Easy it were to succumb to the siren's melodi-
    ous spell !

Nevertheless we have learn'd to prefer, tho' we
    lose them forever,
    Here to renounce our desires and the lures of
        delight to repel.

" We, the ephemeral, we have attain'd to the
    rapture of giving   .
    Succor to others, yea, life itself, their grief to
        remove ;
Do we not bear with a smile, the duty, oft harder,
    of living ?
    And, tho' ye hide from our search, we guess
        that your nature is Love.
What' must your majesty be, what the unspeak-
    able merit
    Of your seraphic attendants, your children of
        heavenly light,
If not the noblest of men the least of your bliss
    may inherit, —
    Only permitted to worship afar 'twixt a dawn
        and a night ! "

Hush ! from the blossoms of Spring come sweet
    multitudinous voices,
    Whispers of spirits that seem to the eye as a
        bird or a tree ;
Meadow and hills are alive with joy, and the
    heaven rejoices,
    Ecstasy tuneth the lips of the world to a pæan
        of glee.

Wider horizons and borderless skies lift ever be-
  fore thee,
Thou shalt not cower, my soul, whose garment
    is wove by the sun !
Thou, with the world in thy heart, with eternity
    hovering o'er thee,
Thou and the Spring and thy hope, and the
    Fountains of Being, are one.

THE AMERICAN.

To fare with giants was my fate ;
I understood no word they said,
But trembled at their grisly mien
  And fear'd their crushing tread.

They heeded not the timid dwarf,
They did not hearken when he cried,
But ran their circuits night and day,
  And mighty was their stride.

I learn'd their fatal path to shun,
I watch'd their labor and its ends,
Till by-and-by I had no fear,
  And they became my friends.

They 've builded me a lordly home,
They 've brought me gifts from earth and
    skies,
And what was once a wilderness
  Is now a paradise.

And now, when I would journey forth,
I call the fleetest to my side,
He lifts me to his shoulder broad —
   'T is mine, the giant's stride!

CONSTANCE.

WHENEVER gentle thoughts would nest
They fly to my Belovèd's breast;
Sooth'd on her heart they sleep and wake,
Like swans upon a placid lake.
When lovely wishes are astir
For our delight, they visit her;
They shine their meaning thro' her eyes,
And in her smiles paint Paradise.

I watch her thro' the orchard pass,
And thro' the waving upland grass, —
The very clover loves her foot,
And not a bird to her is mute!
Now she has gone behind the hill,
And yet, methinks, I see her still,
Upon her gracious mission bent —
To bring the sick encouragement.

Now she has reach'd the cottage-door,
And now has cross'd the threshold o'er:
What sudden radiances illume
The dying farmer's darken'd room?
What music lulls his drowsy ears,
As her consoling voice he hears?

He murmurs, " Wife, at last is come
The angel that will lead me home."
   From *Hesper : A Dramatic Poem.*

THE VIOLIN'S COMPLAINT.

HONEST Stradivari made me:
With the gift of love he blest me ;
Once, delight, a master play'd me,
Love awoke when he caress'd me !

Oh the deep, ecstatic burning !
Oh the secrets low and tender !
Oh the passion and the yearning
At our love's complete surrender !

Heartless men, so long to hide me
With the costly toys you cherish ;
I 'm a soul — again confide me
To a lover, ere I.perish !
   From *Hesper : A Dramatic Poem.*

THE POLITICIAN: A PORTRAIT.

WE thought that the plea of a mendicant purse
  was estopt,
 Our comrade was rich, not a briber could sully
  his hand ;
The callow unwittingly fall in the snares of the bad,
 But he had been train'd by the best, with the
  best he would stand.

"Go forth like to David," we cried, "on the glo-
rious path,
And smite with the pebble of Right the giant of
Gath ! "

He brought the high promise, and Fortune her
requisite gifts —
Wealth, learning, and rank ; so the issue, we
reckon'd, was clear ;
He quoted the words which are wine to the hearts
of the brave :
We saw him equipt with the Truth, and depart
without fear.
" Go forth with our blessing ! " we cried ; " tho'
our numbers be few,
They who fight without fear for the right shall
have strength to subdue ! "
He went — and he barter'd his soul : not by
blunder or bribe —
Not even a sin that were genial to plead for his
shame ;
Our foes were a thousand and we but a score ;
he was vain —
And they had but to tickle his ears by shouting
his name :
In a moment was forfeit the terrible strength of
the just ;
We despise and his wicked allies are too wary to
trust.

Hereafter no league will we strike with the plausible men
Whom the shouts of Philistines or flattering
words can restrain :
But send us a Lincoln, so earnest, so simple and
true,
Too poor to be tempted by riches, too proud to
be vain,
Who spurneth the flippant success and the popu-
lar breath,
And will fight for the triumph of Right, unvan-
quisht till death.

THE SECRET OUT.

" ONLY the manner avails ! " daintily urg'd Dil-
ettante.
" Nay, the matter is all ! " Philosopher curtly
replied.
Then came Genius, and wrought in masterful
fashion a marvel :
" Lo ! *my* wisdom is prov'd ! " each of the dis-
putants cried.

THE GIFTS OF THE FATES.

WHEN I was born, the Fates inscrutable,
Who do the will of Providence in men,
Came where I slept, and brought their awful
    gifts.

First lean'd the Eldest over me, and said,
" This seed, my child, Desire-of-Truth is call'd.
I plant it in thee ; with thy growth 't will grow,
And sweet and bitter shall its harvests be, —
Bitter, and sweet, and fleeting.   It will bear
The plenteous apples of Philosophy,
Red-cheek'd and fair, but tainted at the core;
And from it thou shalt pluck the grapes of
    Art,
Which of themselves can never slake thy thirst ;
And all the fruits of Science spring from it, —
Eat them thou shalt, with hunger unappeas'd.
But ever must thou wait the coming crop
To satisfy thy wants.   This is my gift."
She paus'd, and sow'd the seeming-tiny seed.

The second Sister, with the mien of one
Who mocks, pretending friendship, smil'd, and
    said,
"Let my boon, little godson, make thee great !
Let it incite thee to excel, to soar
And sing above thy fellows ! "   And she blew
Ambition's orient bubble in my brain.

Then the third Sister, in whose haggard face
The wreck of beauty swam the waves of age,
Came to the cradle, look'd at me, and stopp'd,
As one that bears irrevocable news
Delays awhile to tell them.   When she spoke
A lover's pity trembled in her words :
" Life's youngest hope ! my benison to thee !
Pilgrim and waif, too soon the knowledge comes
That Earth is vast and lonely.   For thy mate
A woman's Image in thine inmost soul
Indelibly I cut ; nor Time nor thou
May blot it out or mar.   Be it thy lot
To wander thro' the world and seek a face
To match thy soul's presentment.   By decree,
These eyes shall haunt thee when thou fath-
    omest
The dark or hazel eyes of half a race
Of women ; and distinctly from these lips,
Tho' Folly lure thee and tho' Circe tempt,
A voice shall speak — *My lover, come away,* —
Till thou shalt turn and listen.   Books and
    throngs,
The stress of circumstance and pride of power,
And the strong urge of emulous desire
To trample evil for another's good, —
These shall detain thee, but they may not keep.

" Thy baffled yearning haply may create
In casual friend the semblance of thy Love, —
A pitiful illusion !   Sad, like it
The shadowy counterpart thy restless mind

May conjure from his hopes, and designate
To be in fancy worship'd for the true, —
This lifeless changeling shall thy passion scorn.
Amid the heat of spectral merriment
Oft thou shalt feel, but vaguely guess the cause,
Cold, sudden pangs, as for a world bereav'd ;
Tears thou shalt shed that thine estate, the Earth,
Is but a film ensphering emptiness,
Which   lately   seem'd   an   empire,   boundless,
        bright,
Where Hope might mate him with heroic deeds,
And splendid enterprise might kindle Will
To glory, as the sunshine kindles ocean.
Nay, even in thy triumphs thou shalt grieve,
And sigh the cheapness of success that lifts
Thee nothing nearer her.   Yet evermore,
Above the victory, beyond despair,
Her smile shall teach reproof, encouragement.
At night, beneath the solemn stars and moon,
Thou shalt have inklings that thy Lady lives ;
In forests dim, across the sea's repose,
By vales of noon and ever-youthful brooks,
Contented lakes, and islands slumberous,
And   on   the   mountains   which   outspread   their
        slopes
To hoard the golden bounty of the sun,
Thy heart shall cry, *She lives !*   The birds shall
        sing
Their hints of her ; the flowers murmur, *Haste,*
But now our Sister pass'd !   Thou shalt believe
The poets are her prophets ; thou shalt start

To hear her voice when violin or flute
Wafts notes ineffable on Music's tide ;
And when dead Beauty looketh down on thee
From out the fading past, as angels smile
Upon believers thro' the Future's veil,
Thou shalt exclaim, *'T is she ! The painter saw
Or dream'd my Love ! I may not rest ! On !
On !*

" This, darling, is the destiny I grave
Upon thine inmost soul.   Thy quest shall be
The pattern of this Image.   Thou shalt seek
Thro' all the dark and open ways of life,
Retreat, repose, despair prohibited ;
And often shalt thou think of Death itself
As of a stream upon whose farther bank
This Form elusive, beautiful, and dear
Thou shalt pursue no more." — She softly kiss'd
My lips, and then departed with her mates.
The babe slept on, unconscious of his doom.

PERFECTIBILITY.

GOD first made man of common clay
And o'er the Earth he brute-like went;
But deep within his bosom stirr'd
A strange, unearthly discontent.

Woman God made a living soul —
He made her fair, he made her sweet, —

Upon her with delight man look'd,
And brought his conquests to her feet.

In her he found his heart's desire ;
He lov'd, and was no more a clod ;
Subtly she purifies his soul,
Surely she draws him up to God.

DEPARTURE.

My feet no more this path shall tread
Which thro' the changes of the year
To one unchanging welcome led,
To converse high and hearty cheer :
The weeds shall choke her lilies' bed
    And hide the violets here.

This path shall vanish like a wake
Upon the lonely, restless sea,
And here no dawn again shall break
On eyes that shone with joy for me :
As hearts have lov'd, so must they ache —
    O sad mortality !

DESIDERIA.

TWENTY years hence, when all is done, —
If Time not sooner set me free, —
Some may speak of a battle won :
What were a world of praise to me ?

Grant the proudest that might befall, —
Marble-cold is the laurel'd brow ;
Friends, wealth, fame ?   I would give them all,
Soul of my soul, for thy love *now !*

UNWORTHINESS.

WHEN I remember what I am
   And what I know my Love to be,
I tremble lest some day she grieve
   My large unworthiness to see.

O Love, if e'er this grief befall,
   I pray thee, pity and forgive :
By thy sweet grace and purity,
   If thou still love, I 'll learn to live.

OVERHEARD IN HADES.

LIKE the miser in whose hoard
Not a dollar for spending is stor'd,
Death the ravenous, Death the base,
Munch'd and sulk'd in charnel-place,
And tho' battening ever was never content,
But whin'd to himself this grim lament :

" Shall I ne'er conquer in the strife
I wage with my niggardly rival, Life?
Fed only as it may suit his will,
Must I go hungry and thirsty still?

My craving can never glutted be
Until a mortal shall come to me
In preference to my haughty foe.
Cold are the victuals he drops below!
Scornfully into my larder he flings
Peasants and statesmen, priests and kings,
But not till the epicure, greedy and sly,
Has suck'd their marrow and juices dry.

" Odd are the antics they play in the sun
As they try to cover their carrion !
One swaddles his body in purple and gold,
And his fellows in thraldom he may hold ;
One dons three crowns and petticoats low,
And multitudes gather to kiss his toe ;
Another has buckled a sword at his side
And over the heads of a people may ride ;
A choker of white and a broadcloth coat
Peculiarly virtuous virtues denote ;
By a mantle of silk or a jacket of wool,
You shall know a judge from a common fool.
The Tailor is lord of the lords of the Earth,
Tho' all men are equal — and naked — at birth ;
Two arms, two legs, a paunch and a head —
That is the sum of the regalest dead !
A bucket of water with crimson hue,
Of bones and ashes a quintal or two —
What mortal has more ?   Their glory and love
They leave, when they die, in their wardrobe
above.

" I have folded and fondled in my arms
Voluptuous Cleopatra's charms,
For which kings fritter'd a world away, —
I found them only a tawnier clay ;
And large-ey'd children have hither come,
Whose pallid cheeks and lips so dumb
Their mothers have kiss'd in a blind despair,
As if the sources of bliss were there,
And I have kiss'd in the self-same spot —
If bliss was there, I tasted it not ;
I 've heard a desperate maid implore
To clasp her lover an instant more,
I 've seen a husband by night and by day
Watch his belovèd wither away —
How his hope would sink and mine would rise
At her waning strength and glassing eyes !
Fathers have offer'd their treasure to me
If I would but set their darlings free ;
And I have marvel'd at friends so true
That, parted, no smiles the living knew :
Yet tho' in the sun these precious seem'd
All equally worthless them I esteem'd ;
Whether fat or lean, whether young or old,
All tasted clammy, insipid, and cold,
To my immemorial appetite ;
I found no more pith nor smack of delight
In the dainty babe that dies at birth
Than in shrivel'd Methuselah's juiceless earth.

" But Life feasts ever on winy blood
And tissues that glow in a passionate flood :

While even the sick, by pangs distraught,
And even the sad, with anguish fraught,
And even the bad, whom remorse pursues,
Instead of me would my rival choose.
Only the fool, whose wits are unstrung,
Or the criminal rogue, by terror stung,
Would hasten his violent term's surcease —
Not loving me, but in search of peace.

" Once to my ears the murmur of Fame
Whisper'd a terrible Conqueror's name :
He had sent so many messengers o'er
From the thick of battle, a million or more,
That I look'd to him as a dear ally,
And hungrily waited for him to die.
One night, when the Earth was shaken by storm,
Hither was wafted my Emperor's form —
A godlike forehead, a parchment cheek,
Mouth pinch'd, eyes sunken, and eagle beak ;
And this, forsooth, was my long-sought prize !
More succulent is each beggar that dies.

" Once, once, I deem'd my victory near,
And to greet a willing visitor here :
For a Pessimist proud, of lancet wit,
Condemn'd the world, after probing it,
And declar'd — oh, sweetest of human breath !
That better, far better than Life is Death.
He emptied the vials of his scorn
Over a universe forlorn,
Which easily might have been Paradise

If somebody only had ask'd his advice,
Instead of a blundering, broken machine,
Which must be forever because it has been,
Unable to pause for oil or repairs,
Crushing and killing the puppets it bears.
How it chanc'd that a creature so wise was cre-
    ated
By lunatic force, has never been stated ;
But I relish'd his wisdom and did n't inquire
If my sage philosophe had a fool for his sire.
He prov'd there 's no basis for hope nor for joy,
And that to *exist* means just to *destroy*,
Since all things, as he infallibly saw,
Must feed blind Will's insatiate maw.
But most he hated and most despis'd
His groveling fellowmen, who priz'd
Their tyrant Life — the coward crew
Who shut their eyes to the real and true,
Call evil good, call torment bliss,
And crawl on their trembling knees to kiss
The hand that smites, — for mercy plead
From the demon himself, who their woe de-
    creed, —
Who ask forgiveness for sin and wrong
That not to *them* but to *him* belong, —
And pray that forever, having died,
They may strum their harps his throne beside.
' Vile dupes and cringers,' my Pessimist quoth,
' Cowards and hypocrites, tho' I am loth,
' The core of my wonderful secret to tell,
' I 'll give you a hint; so, ponder it well.

' We all can make our martyrdom less
' By returning at once into Nothingness.
' In sterile sorrows our years why spend
' To reach, by misery's zig-zag, the end
' To which with a step we can instantly cross,
' Now and forever ?   Existence is loss,
' Constant and imbecile ; let us die,
' For death, only Death can satisfy !
' Let us play one joke on insolent Fate,
' And out of his wilderness emigrate ;
' Not a man remain to suffer his curse
' While the bungling scheme jolts from bad to
  worse.'

" So I thought, ' At last joy seeketh me ! '
And I watch'd my sapient spokesman, but he,
Tho' oft from his lips pour'd out my praise,
Was greedy of living many days.
No Sadducee ever more tightly clung
To Life, than he of the lying tongue ;
The flattery of men he sought,
And every callow disciple brought
A vulgar pleasure to his conceit ;
And loudest he preach'd that I am sweet
When most his selfish desires he fed ;
And he damn'd Life hardest when Death he
  fled ;
Until, at three score two and ten
This lifelong hypocrite, vilest of men,
Died, and his corpse I hurried to pitch
To the maggots and rats in yonder ditch.

"And still I starve, and may feel no joy
Till a willing mortal I hither decoy;
While Life is as jubilant now as when
He began his pastime of making men.
I cannot conceive what sport there is
In crowding Hades with carcases!"

PRISONERS.

EVERYWHERE the sculptor hears
A voice unheard by other ears;
It half commands and half entreats,
As this burden it repeats:
"Hasten, master! quickly come!
Countless ages, dark and dumb,
Frozen in this prison white
Has my beauty long'd for light.
Hasten! with thy chisel keen
Cut away my marble screen,
And before your gladden'd eyes
See a perfect statue rise!"

So at times I strangely hear
Messages distinctly near,
"Tarry not! I would be free!"
Whisper lips well known to me.
"Silence deeper than the tomb,
Darkness raven as the gloom
Wrapping the decrees of Fate,
Here surround me as I wait.
Hasten, hasten to set free
Thy perfect self that is to be!"

FAME.

" BETTER than all is fame," he said :
   " 'T is better than wealth or wine
To see the populace sway its head
   And to hear its shouts combine !

" Sweeter than kiss the bridegroom sips,
   Is the honey-sweet of fame,
When the grateful nation opens its lips
   To utter a hero's name ! "

Trampled by hoofs and hurrying feet,
   With powder and blood bestain'd,
His body they found, on the foe's retreat,
   Where the bullets thickest rain'd.

Silently thro' the crowded street
   The muffled coffin came ;
Not a word — not a cheer — hearts quicker
     beat, —
   And that was the hero's fame.

VASHTI.

THERE is a pleasure-place surpassing fair,
In lawns abounding and dim bridal bowers ;
All tropic spices and exotics rare
Mingle their fragrance with the sweet wild-flow-
     ers' ;
And from a terrac'd hill gleam haughty towers.

And there are stately trees whose shadows loop
Broad cirques of twilight round their trunks all
     day;
And orchards ever-ripe, whose branches droop
With fruits which feed the eye; and fountains
     play,
Tingeing with fadeless irises their spray.

Pomegranates there, and purple figs and white,
And grapes full-orb'd, with amethystine gloss,
Peep from the leaves and lure the appetite;
Anemones on breezy uplands toss,
And poppies slumber in a windless fosse.

Enchanting beings dwell there at their ease,
Women of queenly stature, dreamy-ey'd,
Who wander pensive o'er the terraces,
Or leisurely thro' copse and meadows glide,
Or float in shallops on a drowsy tide.

Their raiment is of snow-white gossamer,
Which like a nimbus round them vaguely flows,
And undulates responsive when they stir,
Or ripples sinuous over their repose,
And flushes faintly with the body's rose.

Sometimes they bathe them in a placid lake,
And gather lotus-blossoms, or compete
With swift, majestic swans; sometimes they
     make
Fair patterns on the greensward with their feet,
Their skirts far-floating, as they curve and meet.

A purple mist hangs over that demesne,
Such as September breathes among the hills,
Dreamy, delightful; and from quires unseen
A siren-melody the garden fills
Sweeter than fragrance which a rose distils.

Wistful, I paus'd before the ivied gate,
And roam'd in fancy aisles of high-branch'd
    trees ;
Then spake a soothing voice, " Why hesitate ?
Here is the refuge that from sorrow frees, —
Thine to enjoy are all its joyaunces."

Then stole a Damsel from a thicket near,
And when she came and laid her hand in
    mine,
And whisper'd sweet perdition in my ear,
My pulses tingled as with charmèd wine,
And I was captive to her eyes divine.

She led me unresisting tow'rds the Hall,
And with gay tales our passing entertain'd ;
But if I woo'd, she let her lashes fall,
In startled modesty, and sigh'd, and feign'd
Delicious languor, and my kiss restrain'd.

Her beautiful companions as we pass'd
Hail'd us with smiles, and gleeful music made :
And thus we mounted to the Palace vast
Whose alabaster portals are inlaid
With lazuli and agate, sard and jade.

Golconda 's poorer for the riches there!
Great orient rubies on the threshold burn'd,
And   diamonds   sparkled — each   a   monarch's
          wear —
By me unheeded when the Damsel turn'd
Her lips for kisses, and I, kissing, yearn'd.

How nimbly she her girdle-clasp undid,
Disclosing as the fluttering garment fell
Canova's dream of Helen, — how she hid
Her face upon my breast, I may not tell :
Long is the pow'r of Aphrodite's spell!

Know ye the pangs of unconsuming fire
And burden of much kissing, when ye learn
Satiety is restless as desire,
And habit drives ye to the sin ye spurn,
And deeper loathing is your sin's return?

One eve, beneath our blue-enamel'd roof,
Where hung a mimic moon, and gems were
          set
In artful constellations, — grim, aloof,
I listen'd to the Damsel's canzonet,
Which coil'd around me like an amulet.

She ceas'd, and for a moment neither stirr'd,
But I could feel her sorcery draw near
And lure in will's despite : and then I heard
A Voice that seem'd within me utter clear,
I am Eternal: all is mortal here!

As when Lisbona into Tagus sank
There was a roar of waters and a leap,
A momentary gurgle as they drank
Magnificence which ages toil'd to heap —
Then sunshine's mockery, and silence deep :

So swiftly were those pleasure-haunts destroy'd,
Their pride annull'd, their feres annihilate,
And all their lawns and bosky spaces void :
'Neath murky skies, across morasses great,
Alone I grop'd, appall'd and desperate.

PREMONITIONS.

I.

HAVE you ever felt your heart heave fast,
    And the tears rush into your eyes,
And a sense of victory flood your soul
    As the sunlight floods the skies ?

And you cannot tell why your heart exults,
    Or whence those sweet tears rise ;
But you know, tho' you age with a thousand
        worlds,
    That Youth beyond them lies !

II.

Heavenly hours that mark the passing
    Of the couriers of Truth !
Premonitions that the future
    Shall fulfil the vision — Youth !

Thoughts elusive and so dainty
   That they scarcely kiss the mind, —
Kiss, and flee e'er we can clasp them,
   Leaving ecstasy behind!

TO TRUTH.

GOADED by fears, by doubts perplex'd,
By rival gusts of logic vex'd,
Baffled by *whither, whence,* and *why,*
To thee, O Truth, to thee I cry!

Hide not thy wormwood-nippled breast —
Quenchless my thirst, life-old my quest!
O hide no more, but satisfy,
Tho' I grow drunk or mad, or die!

MANKIND'S HIGHEST.

A DREAM entic'd the Spirit of the Earth,
And as, in sleep, fantastic shapes he chas'd,
The Hours slumber'd and the Laws delay'd.
When he awoke, behold! man's puny race
He found had in the fleeting interval
Expir'd as silently as bubbles burst.
A smile of pity cross'd the Spirit's lips:
"To think the weaklings, if I nodded, died!
But after all," he said, "the tiny imps
Have startled from me many a hearty laugh.

My time would drag could I no longer see
The shifting scenes of Human Comedy."
So men he made anew : and that the new
Might nowise differ from the elder breed,
He hunted 'mid the ruins of the past
A book wherein true types of men are drawn ;
And from those patterns he repeopled Earth.
Upon that book, my Shakespeare, was thy name.

ELEGY

ON A LITTLE FRIEND WHO WAS DROWNED.

MOURN not for those who die in youth : the
    splendor
Of day's beginning lighted all they knew ;
For them no tale of losses, no surrender,
    Nor the long struggle to be simply true.

The sun, the stars, the shimmer of the ocean
    Were wonders still, not yet too often seen ;
Life to young eyes is heightened by emotion —
    The goal, how fair ! unguess'd the toil be-
       tween.

They heard of noble deeds, and long'd to do
    them,
    Sure that their wish should all they wish'd
      possess ;
The magnet pow'r of antique heroes drew them ;
    The best they lov'd, nor dreamt the world
      gives less.

We, we must age, but in our recollection
  Forever young, forever bright, they shine !
From death they took the last supreme perfec-
      tion
  Of souls untarnish'd by the soul's decline.

Mourn not for them : wherever be the sources
  Of love and gladness, thither have they gone ;
And infinite, like hope's, are now their courses,
  And theirs the beauty of eternal dawn.

MIDWINTER WISHES.

O TO lie in the ripening grass
That gracefully bends to the winds that pass,
And to look aloft, the oak-leaves through,
Into the sky so deep, so blue !

O to feel as utterly free
As the oriole swinging above on the tree,
Or the locusts piping their drowsy whirr,
Or the down that sails from the thistle-burr !

O to float with the cloudy drifts,
Changing hue as the sunlight shifts,
Or hastening gaily into the West
To follow the blushing sun to rest !

O for the secret of Nature's power
To drain the joy of the present hour !
O to work and glow in the sun !
O to sleep, when the day is done !

WEST AND EAST.

WHEN my soul darkens at the time's disgrace, —
The pious cant of rogues in public place,
Private debauch, and wolfish, mad pursuit
Of joyless wealth, all genial voices mute, —
From our too sordid, sensual West I turn
To the rapt East, where mystic dreamers yearn.

Speechless, astonish'd, worshiping they brood
Before the vision of Infinitude —
The Spirit Everlasting, in whose sight
The constellated splendors of the night
Are but as dew upon the morning grass,
A moment's sparkle, ere they drop and pass.

To souls transfigur'd by this glimpse sublime
What were desires whose purpose ends in Time?
To hearts communing with Eternal Power
What were the mundane triumphs of an hour,
Or service of the senses?   Pleasure, pain,
And all that dims that vision, they disdain.

SOLIDARITY.

SHEPHERD on Dakota's hills
    When you drive your flock to shearing,
Sailor on the Carib Sea
    As your ship is southward steering,

Guess ye where the goal may be?
Fleece and freight shall come to me,
Spite of distance and of veering.

Hands shall pass, but none shall keep
Till into the hand intended
Drop the unknown brother's gift,
And the service-chain be ended.
Spin and weave, then! sow and reap,
Drive the furrow thro' the deep,
Work of one with all is blended.

Cease the feud of hand and brain!
Tell me, which in worth exceeded,
Who first made the duty plain,
Or who best the duty heeded?
No true worker works in vain,
Each shall have his wage again,
All are noble, all are needed.

NOCTURNE.

O NIGHT of infinite power and infinite silence and
space,
From you may mortals infer, if ever, the scope
divine!
The jealous Sun conceals all but his arrogant
face,
You bid the Milky Way and a million suns to
shine.

Each star to numberless planets gives light and
    motion and heat,
But you enmantle them all, the nearest and
    most remote ;
And the lustres of all the suns are but spangles
    under your feet, —
Mere bubbles and beads of noon, they circle
    and shine and float.

TO ———.

STAND there a moment, while the sun
Touches thy hair !   Lift, lift those eyes divine
Until they look in mine, —
So ! — I would clasp thee in embrace
Death-proof, and feel thy face
And breast and form melt, mingle, intertwine,
Till Mine and Thine
Were one, forever one !

UNREQUITED PASSION.

THE roses climb over the trellis,
    And blush at the sun's warm kiss,
The meadow-grass sports with the South wind,
    The little birds carol their bliss :
O lisp not of love, little blossoms,
    O cease, little birds from your glee ;
Your joy only sharpens my anguish,
    There is never more love for me.

Instead of your gayness that mocks me,
  'T were easier far to bear
The grimmest of all the aspects
  That Nature in anger can wear, —
Some swift and awful convulsion
  That shatters the earth in twain,
When man, as he dies defiant,
  Forgets his impotent pain!

THE HYMN OF FORCE.

I AM eternal!
  I throb thro' the ages;
I am the master
  Of each of Life's stages.

I quicken the blood
  Of the mate-craving lover;
The age-frozen heart
  With daisies I cover.

Down thro' the æther
  I hurl constellations;
Up from their earth-bed
  I wake the carnations.

I laugh in the flame
  As I kindle and fan it;
I crawl in the worm;
  I leap in the planet.

Forth from its cradle
  I pilot the river;
In lightning and earthquake
  I flash and I shiver.

My breath is the wind;
  My bosom the ocean;
My form's undefin'd;
  My essence is motion.

The braggarts of science
  Would weigh and divide me;
Their wisdom evading,
  I vanish and hide me.

My glances are rays
  From stars emanating;
My voice thro' the spheres
  Is sound, undulating.

I am the monarch
  Uniting all matter;
The atoms I gather,
  The atoms I scatter.

I pulse with the tides,
  Now hither, now thither;
I grant the tree sap;
  I bid the bud wither.

I always am present,
  Yet nothing can bind me;

Like thought, evanescent,
They lose me who find me.

BEREFT.

AT night, in the haunts of slumber,
Wakeful I lie and weep,
For the burden of loss is upon me
And will not let me sleep.

Far off, the desolate ocean
Utters its old refrain —
The sigh of eternal passion,
The sob of eternal pain.

THE CHASE AND NOT THE QUARRY CHARMS.

CALM was the woodland as at dawn:
Perdu amid its stillness, I
Dream'd open-ey'd, when lo, a fawn
Went softly sauntering by.

Her skin was dappled, sleek, and fair,
Her form was joyous to behold ;
She brows'd and hearken'd with an air
Half timorous, half bold.

It was a witching sight to see
Above the ferns her lovely head,

So tame, and yet so proud and free !
    She spied me — trembled — fled !

The pulses of my will took fire,
And every thought my being through
Was molten to a sole desire,
    That creature to pursue.

Long, long the chase ! no swallow swoops
So swiftly o'er a rippled lake,
As she just brush'd the startled troops
    Of evergreen and brake.

But if I paus'd for lack of breath,
Or if I slak'd me at a brook,
Like one who subtly maddeneth,
    She too would pause and look.

Long, long the chase ! At last prevail'd
My stronger sinews, stauncher will ;
Upon a mossy bank she fail'd,
    Frighten'd, but tame and still.

I bent to stroke her glossy head,
When, wonder ! by a sudden spell,
My dappled beauty gone — instead,
    A beauteous damosel.

She lur'd me with her lustrous eyes,
She seem'd part eager, part afraid ;
" I am the dauntless lover's prize,
    My will is thine," she said.

Her beauty lighted up the wood,
Her cheeks were joyful as the dawn, —
But drew me not, for I pursued
    In fancy still the fawn.

IREM.

THE Arab dreams in his tent
Of Irem, the Beautiful City,
Which as a child he was told
His ancestors builded of marble :
He dreams, and a yearning for home —
For the life unspent in the desert,
For the shady repose of the courtyard,
The tinkle and flash of the fountain,
And voice of friends at the threshold, —
Stirs in his heart and awakes him.
There, thro' the folds of his tent,
He sees along the horizon
The minarets gleaming and domes
Of Irem, the Beautiful City,
Of Irem, the home of his dream !
Mount not, Arab, thy steed,
Be not the dupe of the desert!
See the mirage, how it fades !
Never may mortal attain
To the gate of beautiful Irem.

I too, I too have beheld,
When all but the ache in my heart

Lay quiet in sleep, I have seen
The deeps of my spirit unveil,
And a Beautiful City beyond them.
Its walls and its spires are caught
In the flush of the splendor of dawn,
And the fragrance of June is afloat,
From the blossoming trees in the streets.
I hear the laughing companions,
I hear the voice of the mother,
And down from the steps of her home,
She comes, my Soul's Desire,
She comes, with a welcoming hand,
With love on her lips, and a song.
Fain would I speak, but for sobs —
Fain would I look, but my eyes
Are blurr'd with tears, and the Vision
Fades in the mist of grief.

Sweet, sweet, sweet,
Tender and sad and sweet,
In the desert at noon the mirage
Which memory paints on the soul,
Of Irem the City of Morning,
The home of the hopes of our Youth.

REVERIE.

SWEET is it over shelving sands to stroll
When the victorious tide begins to lose,
And watch the stubborn-yielding billows roll,

Or look upon the mid-sea's scudding hues, —
Sweet is it then to loiter and to muse.

The keel of *Argo* cut that furrow there
When Jason cried " To Colchis " !   This spent
    foam
Was Aphrodite's pillow ; mermaids fair
Adorn'd them with this sea-weed in their home,
Where coral-forests bloom and dolphins roam.

Now wroth Achilles to Poseidon tells
His grievances and retribution vows ;
Now the last eloquence of Athens swells
Above the mob of breakers ; here carouse
The fair-hair'd Argives near their ruddy prows.

Here rise the saucy, unobsequious waves
To wet the sandals of the Danish king ;
Here spectral pirates crawl from nameless graves
And count again their booty, quarreling ;
And here Pizarro draws the fatal ring.

Columbus kneels exultant, and unfurls
The cognizance of Christ and Ferdinand ;
Here weeping mothers and bewilder'd girls
Cry out " God speed ye ! " to the *Mayflower*
    band,
Long after sails are hidden from the land.

And Bonaparte here reconstructs his doom,
Reversing Waterloo, or peers afar

Till Breton cliffs along the horizon loom
In bitter-sweet mirage ; this sodden spar
Bore Nelson's duty-sign at Trafalgàr.

Flotsam and jetsam of o'erladen Time,
Wash'd on the strand where Fancy musing goes !
The waves ebb'd with my dreams, and now
  reclimb
The glistening slope, a wild Northeaster blows,
And on the sea its frothy mantle throws.

THE REFORMER.

This is, O Truth, the deepest woe
 Of him thou biddest to protest ;
With men no kinship may he know, —
 Thy mission hems from worst and best.

The wolf that gauntly prowl'd the wood
 From human kind more mercy got,
Than he who leads men to their good,
 And stands alone, yet flinches not.

Thou grantest not one friendly hand,
 Or heart, on which he may rely ;
Alone and dauntless must he stand,
 Alone must fight, alone must die !

ENVOI.

I WALKED with poets in my youth,
  Because the world they drew
Was beautiful and glorious
  Beyond the world I knew.

The poets are my comrades still,
  But dearer than in youth,
For now I know that they alone
  Picture the world of truth.

www.ingramcontent.com/pod-product-compliance
Lightning Source LLC
Chambersburg PA
CBHW030541270326
41927CB00008B/1471